After Spell

Library of Congress Cataloging-in-Publication Data

Van Winckel, Nance.
    After A Spell : poems_ / by Nance Van Winckel.
    p.   cm.
    ISBN 1-881163-24-5 (alk. paper). — ISBN 1-881163-25-3
(pbk. : alk. paper)
    - I. Title.
    PS3572.A546A69 1998   —   97-44333
    811'.54 — dc21   CIP

The paper in this book meets the guidelines
for permanence and durability of the Committee
on Production Guidelines for Book Longevity
of the Council on Library Resources.∞

Printed in the U.S.A.

9 8 7 6 5 4 3 2 1

The Miami University Press Poetry Series
General Editor: James Reiss

The Bridge of Sighs, Steve Orlen
People Live, They Have Lives, Hugh Seidman
This Perfect Life, Kate Knapp Johnson
The Dirt, Nance Van Winckel
Moon Go Away, I Don't Love You No More, Jim
Simmerman
Selected Poems: 1965-1995, Hugh Seidman
Neither World, Ralph Angel
Now, Judith Baumel
Long Distance, Aleda Shirley
What Wind Will Do, Debra Bruce
Kisses, Steve Orlen
Brilliant Windows, Larry Kramer
After A Spell, Nance Van Winckel

After A Spell

Poems by
Nance Van Winckel

Miami University Press
Oxford, Ohio

Acknowledgments

Thanks to the editors of the journals in which these poems, some in slightly different versions, first appeared:

Alaska Quarterly Review: "My Husband's Whistling"

California Quarterly: "This is Not a Drill"

Chicago Review: "I Forget Myself"

Columbia: "Culling Lentils"

Crazyhorse: "Black Jacket, Black Pants, Black Motorcycle"

The Denver Quarterly: "Last Trip to Balfour" and "Cockadoodledoo"

High Plains Literary Review: "Here's Hoping for One More Snow" and "A Queen for Every Rock & Roll Kingdom"

Indiana Review: "It"

The New Virginia Review: "Great Blue Heron on the Diving Board" and "Coast"

The Northwest Review: "Two Hungers. John the Baptist," "What Are You Looking At?" "My Sister's Sonnet Was Due Tuesday," and "The Great Aunts Explain the Family Tree"

The Paris Review: "Unfinished Canvas" and "Every Good Thing"

Ploughshares: "The Company We Keep"

Poetry Northwest: "Hurry, Get Up, There's Work to Do," "Par Nothing," and "Mrs. Miller's Miracle" (as "Coincidentally")

Prairie Schooner: "Stoop" and "Going to Kroger's"

Quarterly West: "Our House Was Full without Us" and "Baby & Brain"

The Southern Review: "Injunction"

Talking River Review: "If Pursued, She's Sure She'd Go the Other Way" and "She Cried in Their Arms"

Virginia Quarterly Review: "Do It Yourself Nativity" and "Miniature"

Yarrow: "Two or Three Tables Away"

Grand Mothers (Holt, Rinehart, & Winston): "Going to Kroger's"

Thanks also to Christopher Howell, Elizabeth Kirschner, and, as always, to Rik Nelson, for suggestions on poems in this manuscript.

Table of Contents

I. The Company We Keep

II. This is Not a Drill

III. I Forget Myself

IV. After a Spell

I. The Company We Keep

Hinge

Sonia tells me about Egyptian rulers
    living life after life, each one
        a layer deeper in the earth vaults.

Spirits that block the way down
    have to be sung to, Sonia says.

Now fog over our pea fields lifts.
    And the smoke from our smokes
        goes out to meet it.

The back door whines. A man calls to us
    down the steps: Table No. Nine

wants their check, a crew of diners
    who don't know what to do
        with all the silverware.

We climb the stairs, pass
    through the squeak.

All night we pour and smile,
    stack and clear, our copper bracelets
        jingling. Sonia knows which coins

will have value in the next kingdom.
    Clear and stack. We pour

and smile and say
    the charms. We fill
        our pockets.

She Cried in Their Arms

Before she got on the plane with me
a girl cried in the Hare Krishnas' arms.
The many bells on their bodies
rang through the air.

Beside me in the seat, she's small
in her white gowns, huddled
and occasionally forgetting
to hold back her sobs.

The holy ones outside our window
wave. Their tiny ponytails
signal the big planes higher
and the little ones lower.

When the girl reaches to accept
my last stick of gum, her arms
still bear the old blues of needled
bruises. Whatever ways her former gods

went wrong on her—the piercings
and stigmata from way back—clearly
she's forgiven them, one by one.
The tinkling bells on her ankles

calm down. Her head tilts
toward my shoulder; her eyelids
flutter closed. The further she slumps
into sleep, the harder she falls into me.

Sonia's Last Date
with Calvin Holding Eagle

Or so she says. Her blue eyes
open a path to the water
where I kneel, dip my hand,
drink. She's been crying
and I have doled out the last
useless crumbs of advice.

Bearing down on the lake:
one swan who holds her head
as if not to see us, as if to erase
this whole half of shore, water,
women, and the craggy jaw
of mountain behind them.

A man has told my friend she's
the paler version of someone else
he's loved. So when his fingers press
along the blue veins of her breast,
she's following him there, nearing
something buried and emptied of air.

The gray clouds above take on
the shape of a shipwreck. Half a boat
stuck through the lake. That's what
the swan swims toward: icy planks
of water. Into them, again and again
she'll knock the long burden of her head.

If Pursued, She's Sure
She'd Go the Other Way

Her china cup holds white wine
and an ice cube—a soft chime
in the air before she drinks.

If he tried talking her upstairs
over Lil's, or downstairs where cold
swirls the kegs in a slow orbit,

she'd say No to his face, no to his eyes
that only hours ago held his wife's.
Darker now, his eyes watch rain,

rain loud all night on the tin roof.
He stands by the back door, smoking,
blowing rings toward the trees.

Making their own breeze, darts fly
behind us, whirring past
toward the red scratched eye.

I tell her what she's about to light up
is about to kill her. But she smiles
and touches the flame to the tip.

I Wish I'd Heard
the Song They Were Singing

In the prison yard a mom and dad
walked with their son, their arms linked
through his. Two gray heads and one
dark one. The sky: autumnal on top,
opaque and wintry on the bottom.
No good poems came to my men
all week, but no matter. The week passed.

I hurried out the door, snapping
my parka and nodding to the three
who raised their heads together, in step
and in time, their lips parted
for what must have been the song's last
high note, which they hit and held
a good long while.

Mrs. Miller's Miracle

After lightning struck my backyard tree,
first the girls' gang came, milling about,
speaking their made-up language, wearing
their costumes of an indivisible nation.
Getting up close to Him with their whispers,
they fingered the face in the bark,
the face of the great survivor, Our Savior.

I confess that later I stole three candles
to put in my three street-facing windows
so that everyone would know my house.
This sector of the city locks itself down
in another jittery brown-out. Caterwauls
from the neighbors' dark rooms, and my tree
lifts Its Face toward that call & response.

After the newsmen's pinstripes made
a picket fence around Him, after those spokes
of gray light on my green, and the mini-cam
had rolled up His sad contemplation of *them,*
I knew what would be launched back
at Kingdom Come: that buzzing
in high-frequency on the jet stream.

I've peered into that charred tree husk
and tried to see what else: rat guts,
sprung clockworks, Mr. Okoro's workboots.
Whatall and I don't know—I can't figure
how some *don't* make Him out.
Thorns adorn His bruised temples.

Eyes dart under His bark lids and lashes.

I've said enough to the circling, popping
bulbs. Told them insignia are everywhere,
thick as trees. In my garden's chunk of black
basalt, I see my two dead sons' fists raised.
In my treetop—but only on the iciest January
morning—an enormous city shines, one that's been
named for me, or for someone very like me.

Two or Three Tables Away

She nibbles a forkful of clams
and tells him about five floors
that went down in one fell
swoop. A stack of rubble
in the city's midst. Sleepers
stacked up but dead
to the world of many
sleeping others. He knows
all about it. Says he's seen
the same channel. For once, why
can't they go, just the two of them,
out for a simple meal
and leave disaster behind? He
refolds his napkin into a perfect
practiced square, drops it
on his plate. We've had
this argument for twenty years,
she says over her spoon
heaped with slaw, as if
any building as tall and wide
as the one they've entered
could be reassembled
once it's this far down.

Injunction

My aunt sat crying, her shoulders
slumped forward, shaking—softly,
then not softly. Two sobs and
two more. Her door was ajar and I
shouldn't have stood there watching.

The state's lawyers had the final words:
A great communal experiment had failed.
No child even knew which father
to lay claim to. Which I should never
have heard, though the huge court's door

had swung open too, and I'd witnessed
the little drama play out: three cousins
removed to a family of calm strangers.
I'd see them always that way, like those passed
on—laughing and cooing in a happy limbo.

My aunt's earrings were the sun
and the moon, silver chariots
that soared many months
across well-traveled skies.
She lifted them from her ears

and set them in a china cup, her face
glistening, beautiful in its red streaks.
As I closed her door, she'd been taking up
her brush in a hand that seemed to shake—
though surely that was the mirror's fault.

The Company We Keep
— *for my sister*

1.
The one she loves she hates. And too
late, she says, for the thing love's become
to let her loose from its grip.

They take it to the hills. Green tent
in blue mountains. They'd bought themselves
fishing licenses, and the conversation began

on trout—cutthroat and Dolly V's—names
bruised and asthmatically deep
inside the second then the third pint

of flat gin. And maybe she'd said brown trout
when she'd meant to say brook.
Which is what got him started,

sent his boot across her hip. Though some—
and just now she can't remember which
blotches of purple and which red welts—

came from her own damn fault,
her own tripping, falling, running
in the general direction of the lake.

2.
The loved thing is so punched in
it's beyond them. A deputy tried
to get pictures: pop and flash at her eyes,

her mouth, the wrung flesh of her forearm.

And what she flashed back—a wince,
a shrug, an abandoned stare. Please
won't someone hunt for her glasses. She can't
drive home without them, though I
had the keys, for Christ's sake, in my hand.

Were all her answers to the sheriff's questions
No? Maybe a few were *maybe.*
Or *I suppose. I don't know.* Lake
in the hills. It always eludes us.
Its great slick dark. How weather comes
out of it. And then memory's
weather. The words she wouldn't say
had already fallen under water, syllables
of stones on the bottom's muck.

3.
Four measly tent stakes pulled loose.
Hunched, huddled figure in the hills.
Didn't the fire out there blaze up?
Didn't any of the nearby campers,
anglers, fishwives awaken? Or the lake
rouse itself to flash back at the moonlight?

How much *No* 'til thunder
set its own charge? Made up a rain
and released it? In the tent's huge
gaping puddle: the sleeping bags still tied
in two tight fists. Now she can't see
her glasses among the broken bottles,

wants to hang nothing—*No, nothing*—
out to dry. Did you have them on
when you ran—and listen, the thing
to say now is not *I don't know,* since

in a minute we'll find them, since they're
just waiting to be seen, to be lifted. Here.

4.
There must have been smoke
if there was rain on that campfire.

Smoke disappearing into what
other campers turned over in warm bags

to whisper once and roll their eyes at
in the dark. Don't let us look their way

or stare. It's a private matter, no matter
the noise, the echoes. Don't let us trespass.

Later she could be heard to pull herself
from the lake. To shake out

her bones of melodrama, her shirt
of cliché. Though the lake might fill

and empty itself a couple more times
this millennium, it's half a block of ice

between us in a few months. The cold
that comes out of it goes back in.

Unsettles its stones, inches them deeper
in the muck. They burrow down.

The Great Aunts Explain
the Family Tree

He died in Baltimore. Crack
of a crab boat on invisible boulder.
He died in palatial lodgings at the split end
of Ventura Highway. He died
on the road, strangled by the wind. Died
in the air, smothered by more
of the same. Died in frozen
pond muck. Died in a heaven of gilt-winged
insects. Died from too much schnapps
and poetry, from poking bad ore. Dead
so he could live an afterlife
in our minds. So he could nudge one,
then two, nostrils up through the ice
and breathe us, scrape us out
from under his nails, lick us clean
of the old blue blood sac.
He died in Spokane. He died
in D.C. In Harlem and gay
Paree. He died four thousand years ago
and last night by the silver moon.
It was . . . yes, it was October. Of that
we are mightily sure.

II. This Is Not A Drill

My Sister's Sonnet
Was Due Tuesday

And I said Okay, I'll help, but you have to think
what it's about. *Well, like all poems of the planet,
you know, what else?* Sure, but what do we
know about that? We've got everyone we love
under one roof. We've never even seen—*The heck
we haven't. What about Mrs. Beals' dead baby
by God in that box?* I got my pencil going:
"Barely two feet of pine planks . . . ." *No,
put maple.* Hey, it's a sound thing we're
after. "The lid Mrs. Beals leaned to lift—
barely two feet of pine planks nailed tight
around her great dead gift." *Wait, hold on,
we can't say that. She's a real person, she
knows us. Don't let's mention any names.*

This Is Not a Drill

All night we're out in the parking lot of stalled
    dreams. The last cigarette smoked. Someone
      I think I might one day love has his
        arm about my waist like I'm a
          sure thing. Then the loud alarm:
            an ambulance flashing signals
              at us. We've been blowing
                circles round ourselves.

In real life I marry someone I never dreamed
    I'd love. We sit around the radio getting
      a tornado's coordinates. Until the
        weatherman in his Volkswagen blows
          clear off the town's only hill.
            Garbage cans hit the window—
              glass at our feet. A little
                fear then, but not much.

One afternoon we're long gone in a rowboat.
    Two fish in a bucket, a third getting itself
      unhooked, when we see the water go too far
        one time. It covers the shoreline
          completely: white inch for white
            inch. Okay, we're scared now—
              oars in the oarlocks
                and nowhere to row.

Great Blue Heron
on the Diving Board

My trail out of sleep across wet grass
into careful contemplation
disappears. Ground mist and blue spruce

crowd a thought that tries me
as much as I try it. Then who
sees who first across the hedge

I don't know. Who's trying harder
to think a thought through to its end?
The bird's eyes, slowly they drain loose

their panic. Her huge head tilts
back. Now the bird flaps once
as if to clear her mind, begin again.

> One claw that loves the warm
> dry board, one wing
> that loves the air.

What Are You Looking At?

Our beers' two heads of foam melting
on the bar, barkeep waiting to wipe
the rings away, and some man staring at me
from across the room. Which my lover
didn't like. We'd had too much heat
for one day, lost there in the Mojave,
which thrilled me, not having come yet
to any real reckoning of fear. Except of
losing him back to his wife. I wasn't afraid
even of the few punches it'd take
to gouge a man's jaw off kilter, only
embarrassed by the one appearing there
as me. I'd just washed my face in the john,
flinging handfuls of cold water
over my eyes, which were greened-up
from the grit. Jeans snug as another skin.
So I may have seemed, for that single
evening, the sort of woman a man, drunk
and tired after a week of overtime, looks at
wrong. Turned up, the song twanged, notes
all around more as a laughter
than a music. Then he said it again and
louder, with an emphasis on the *you,*
as if the onlooker were so different
from the two of us, who'd come down to Moab
to stare at rocks and sun, everything
out there, outside us. I never got to lift
the glass that calmly dripped on the bar,
though my hand stayed just inches away—

my hand reaching to drink,
but waving instead, lamely, in the air,
then both hands waving, trying to signal
Stop. Please. Stop.

A Queen for Every
Rock & Roll Kingdom

The music threw our arms up
then tipped our heads back
with its low taps. We were a crowd
crushing closer. Strung out and
strung together, bodies pressed
into one mass—black and blue
all around ourselves. So when I asked
to see more, someone helped me up,
up into the moonlight on someone
else's shoulders. Higher, where
night's been known to handle us
a little better, we who have been
difficult to handle, arrogant and unruly,
agents of other sorts of happiness.

Last Trip to Balfour

I couldn't dream who he was shouting at in his sleep
to *Take that*. Both of us bone-tired in starched sheets.

All day the eyes of big-horned sheep had been on us.
For miles. One side of their rock ledge, and another.

Elk in their foggy stupors looked up when they saw us,
then back to their lips' slow motion across the meadow.

Seemingly more possible here: a wider swath of loving
between us, and between us and others. But for the talk

in town: some newfound religion many can't abide.
It's got its zapped-out, barefoot, bong-eyed, gooney guru—

and *these* are the embers of his church. Now a char
in the wind. Now the tall long-needled pines feel too close,

too near to us all, we who've picked over the rubble,
touched our cheeks with its ash. I slept here

only off and on, and in the last half-doze, put words
into a man's mouth as he lay dreaming beside me.

Par Nothing

One minute you're in your putt: tiny knock
    and roll, roll, roll. The next you're down
        on the ground, the round flat green
            flipped like a pancake. The course

clicks off in a tilt of darkness. You're a smudge
    on the curtain's black hem.

        Lightning strikes—more a belt
        than a bolt. A flap, and it unfolds
        the billion bright sparks: a current
        to shut down your own. Nerves
        so many stakes in the dirt.

Some days you're one person—limber,
    and in the middle of a backswing that pulls
        back and back. A shoulder's arc keeps
            opening. Back some more.

And some days you're two: green girl
    of the ever-widening swing, and girl

        on her knees in a downpour,
        face in too much too-wet
        grass, tasting rain, tasting
        terror, the one who won't
        completely return to her senses.

Others nod, agree: many are felled every year.
    The belt drops, and the precious shoes

fly off, fly away. The feet kick out.
Then light returns the sky

as sky. And a few of us stand up again,
but no, not the same few.

My Husband's Whistling

Whenever he calls me, I'm out. I'm in back
burying brown bulbs. I dig and dump
and make a row by the barn. Whatever's about
to grow there, who can say for sure?

Next his song slips out the back door.
Then the back door closes. I don't know
the tune. Bucketful of windfall apples
on a stoop; bees under secret orders circling.

Dusk and its entourage, orbiting the orchard,
cannot contain themselves. Say one apple falls;
say it's so ripe it splits. From inside drop two small
seeds, once still, but now aroused from stillness.

Stoop

A man's white underwear in morning
sunlight. He can't get any farther
than his bottom porch step. Cigarette

in hand. An exclamation mark
without the dot: he's
misplaced his matches.

Disastrous news—its faces bleed
into the grass. The paper's too far
to step to, barefoot, in the dew.

Gray aluminum awning over this pale
pause, and a sense of the hedges waiting
for his brief bow on that little stage.

On his bicep a ship
unfurls tall sails, tattoos a blue
on the last cool air of the day.

Hurry, Get Up, There's Work to Do

9 a.m., then 10, and still no sign of her,
the old woman, who every day, early and
limping up my hill, comes to gather
pinecones. Never to look at me or speak,
though it's my fence she climbs over,
my bean patch she walks through
to drift among the dry pines' droppings.

When she appears, a second me stays
at the window, waving to her back.
While the first me goes on sucking up
cobwebs through a hose; the third lingers
over a recipe, a stew, a sauce, an aroma
to blow my house completely off, to Crete—
and there to be a bright shell on the sand.

Wearing her red baseball cap, black sneakers,
the old woman's all set. She knows
a good cone from a bad. She picks
pine needles loose, shakes off a leaf,
a moth's wing. Her son has told me she's
crazy, but Okay, she's out there in the air.
She fills a white sack three feet high.

And No, the daughter has said, they're not
pinecones for wreaths—gold-flecked;
nor for ornaments—sequined. But for
her mother's fire of an afternoon: yellow
crack and high squeal of the quick
burn. Not kindling, but the real thing,

the tall blaze and the wild flame.

Today's wind blows a million pinecones
into the everywhere where she is not.
And when a low cloud moves, it isn't *her*
white sack. My palm print streaks the air
behind the glass. But I've just waved to
no one. To silence and cold. Which makes it
difficult to get down to business.

The second me defies the first, the third
the fourth, and so on. Until one of me takes up
the task: right arm to the wrench. A shoulder-shove
and grunt get the connection made. Sweet
stupid success: the snap and vroom.
So now a current runs through—blue
in the blue wires and red in the red.

III. I Forget Myself

It

Friends in the willows. Friends
in the box shrubs. I was the one
who went after. Reaching
a hand toward an arm. My steps
could snap a branch or crack
a black vine. Then what? Touch
my fingers to my sister's arm?
Make the river stop in its tracks?

High smog over moonlight. A dozen
fireflies half-lit everyone's pose.

How long could we stand motionless
as blue fir trees? Old winds,
under a spell of obligation, stir up
from nothing. The river never rolled
that slowly again. My sister's foot
shot ahead. Nothing in space alone
or in time is so tireless. An arm, held
still aloft, is no one's we'll remember.

Here's Hoping for One More Snow

Though the household's others—aunts, mother,
sister—think this last 26 inches
hasn't long to go. They've got their minds
on what's deeper down and creeping
up: nubs of the green shoots. Out a window

they look past me, my shovel raised in salute,
and past the red tail of my winter cap, a cocoon
for my long braid. The sky's shaker lid
just dropped off, and down went
the white—poured out in a heap.

It's the cure for my sassiness, stifler
of my street-talk, my high-sworn oaths
on the wind. The others think spring means
to include them: their red reopened
into a velvet, a fragrance of roses.

They get a big pot boiling, then weave in
and out through its hooks of steam.
They've just bought crabs from a peddler
who crossed from the coast in a blizzard.
He knocked on our door, and was gone.

He called me boy, and was gone.
The women are foolish. They believe
whatever swam into a man's net yesterday
can cook in their brine today. They open
the door to any knock. They open it a crack.

Taking now my wet mittens and passing me

dry ones: a thumb's crooked stitches we all
know as my aunt's. Long past midnight,
her gnarled knucklebones clatter,
poking the firelight with two blue needles.

When the peddler stood at our door, five
pink-bellied crustaceans in his fist, I shoveled
behind him and around him. Let him
call me the wrong thing. Let half
his face touch the wedge of warmth

through our door, his hand take our money,
one ear hear our laughter, the jokes he'll
never get. In the steaming pot the little crab eyes
roll back. At this hour he's maybe as far
as the mountains that dip down to the sea,

but stalled there by one more snow. Big snow
like a sky all its own. Thin air for a lifetime,
high tundra forever. A bloom of white
enfolds the pass, until the way through
to the other side lies open to dispute.

Coast

Surely my cries woke the late sleepers
of that foreign city. You lay next to me,
moving and stopping inside me
in a certain rhythm. The city
had a sea beside it and a rain
waiting above it. Those waking
turned to their windows.

They saw a tall wave bend down
and stumble shoreward. They heard
a woman's happiness. So far that summer
the days had been hot and dry.
But when a cloud tore open,
the joy that belonged to one
belonged to us all.

Culling Lentils

What our hands feel for
when our eyes look away: the rocks
and dirt, the stems and bugs and scabs.

Twelve women in a blue metal shed.
The army we are in our red bandannas.
Pickers and sorters who've lived before
as madonnas and majorettes.

And every day what'll pass through the sieve
of our hundred fingers—the he said she said
he said. The so many fish in the sea.

Evening fog when we go, morning fog
when we come. *Chop, chop* and *Time's money*—
the same words each driver shouts
down the chute. The black belt unfurls.

November crisp on the dirt clods. And all
we've crossed on our way: rattlesnake in the road,
two wires under a pick-up's hood.

And one more time about what gets in
and hunkers down. Pluck—and *ping*
goes the shriveled seed heart.
Fingers catch and condemn.

And the new girl nodding to the advice
she still regrets, even all these years later,
she didn't take, especially when they'd begged her,
sitting, smoking on the truckless truck seat
out back—to *Let him go, honey, just for us.*

I Forget Myself

Once, after cold creek water had tried all day
    to coax an old stump loose, and after night
had come on as far as the tamaracks, he'd
    finally said it: *Go ahead then, flirt
with me.* I couldn't stand to watch so many stars
    nipping at the creek that way. *Go on,
tell me you don't want my hands here, or here.*

    Just before dark a wind had backed off,
and then the last of the heat. I stood up, brushing
    at the dirt, and walked to the ridge. Below
was everything that had wanted our lives to go
    like this, all of it such a long drop beneath us,
sleepy and small. Now through the tin town
    a red smoke blasted, as a tiny train roared
through: too fast and not about to slow down.

Do It Yourself Nativity
(Woman Escaping from Crèche)

The evening drizzle leaks
under the 1 x 2's. Her blue parka
zipped under blue robes.
She wipes mud from the doll's
eye, turns her back
on the feckless sheep
and knee-high steer.

How did some chicken
cross the road? —That
and its thousand variants—
are Joseph's pastimes.
Until Hark the Herald
ends in a power shutdown.

The sky starless; sun-up
a long way east across
the hilarious highway.
Joe, in thermal socks, drifts
off. Push the baby's cry button.
Let it cry without her.

She'll have herself a good run
toward what's left of the lights.
Nearing the outage, which later
she'll mispronounce as *outrage,*
she slows for a bird carcass
on the blacktop. Supremely busy,
huge ants dismantle it. One by one
tiny feathers cross the road.

Going to Kroger's

As soon as I get behind the wheel
Gran's saying what to touch on the dash
and where to look next. She's blind
and I'm twelve, but this
is an emergency. I back the Studebaker
over a curb and into a street,
where the trees seem so newly sketched,
someone could breeze by
and rub them out with a finger.

Gran says to stop at the end
of this block, and now what
do I see? Just a parade of cars,
I say, with their lights all on,
though it's the middle of an afternoon.
I sit as tall as possible, listening hard
to get this, her story of what makes them
follow the dead around like that.
No one looks my way. No one sees

who sits so well under the big wheel.
They're busy keeping in line behind
their leader, taking turns turning in
beside the stony-eyed angel. Trees
and more trees, and Tell me *what* trees,
Gran wants to know. Everything here
is curbed. Too loud and too many questions.
I can't go any slower, I say, though
the truth was I could. It was all uphill.

She wants to know each house we've passed,

and she's only brought two dollars
for the butter. I'm all she's got,
she tells me, to help her, just this once
and never let's speak of it again. We have
hours to kill, and all she thinks about
are her biscuits. For these she believes
she is loved. She's got a hundred things to do,
but she's only named three or four

when I see the traffic light come from
nowhere to stop us. The red flashes
swallow the car. And What's all
that noise, she's got to know,
while I'm deciding fast how to turn
back from the dizzying stream
of traffic—and My stars, she says,
now you've done it. Now
we're out here on the Avenue.

Species

Big Pine Key, Florida

At the southernmost tip
of their country, an old couple
stood watching the herd
of tiny Key Deer. Spring fawns
left hoofprints the size of dimes
in the sand. In a silence between waves
the woman took the man's hand.
Then the small thunder
of the deer leaving
when the two observers
were seen.

From the boat, a girl with binoculars
who watches all of this
pulls in a sharp breath: the feeling
she's just met herself
going backwards.
The one she loves sleeping late
far below. She takes that hand.

Whatever was vague in their bodies
the heat has pressed in and the sun scalded
until the skin shines.
And all morning two eyes
trained through the black tubes.
The boat bobs, the couple blurs,
and the notion of near-extinction
deepens everyone's joy
when the small deer step out again
from the gnarled mangroves.

Black Jacket, Black Pants, Black Motorcycle

One hand on the gas & thrust of the sky,
one foot on the earth's slow braking,
and all of him coming at me
down a switchback of Mt. Si.
His inner balance interstellar.

Barnacles from a disappeared sea
I'd picked up from the landslide.
Chisel tap and tunk all day—and now
to open my calluses to a cool wind, here,
waving from a boulder at the bottom.

The bloodbath of so much sundown
as if an empire's collapsed between us.
And the road of *him* winding in
and out of view, bringing home
that furious hurried life one of us
loves, and one of us regrets.

Two Sisters Who Have Believed Wishing Hard Brings Apt Results

They've walked these furrows in long
black dresses. Saying wild words

over the wheat sprouts, they've aggravated
water from a dry spring; and surely

they can make our girl's track marks
disappear inch by inch from her arm,

foot by foot from the rug. The sisters'
steely-eyed looks are brief proverbs

and blessings from the Day-book. A man
on TV shows the way. His own hard gaze,

and a humming and a rubbing, bend back
sterling spoons. Two sisters have seen it all.

They hum. They've bent their backbones
to keep the fields smooth, tight as snug sheets.

The TV man has said Phone in *now*
and he'll wish our wishes all the harder.

But the two sisters, having received
the midnight call from the police,

hear the voice of their girl, who's hocked her coat
and is cold and far away and hungry.

Wounded by the terrible ringing,
they drop the phone. Dangling far beneath

the upstairs sisters, it falls to the two who live
below, who take up the receiver and whisper,

It's alright, dear, our other sisters are resting.
They've worked hard wishing the moose calf

down from the foothills, scouring the outrage
of bad blood from a good girl's shoes.

Honey, they're just taking a little lie-down.
So say the coal-bin sisters, their mouths

and stockings indistinguishable from the black
velvet walls. *They're tired now, very tired,*

having hoped our third cousins back
to the homeland, having willed the paperboy out

of the river of forgetfulness, the neighborhood clean
of its smut and sloth and the wrath of ruffians.

IV. After A Spell

Perhaps She'll Say More Tomorrow

— for Sarah Penn Van Winckel, 1956-1992

Tonight the word fired like a bullet
that punctures the whole bulbous
body of the dream. *Sis!* my sister
shouts, and I wake. As if it's time
to put our bikes behind the barn
and wash up. A season of twilight
awaits—after the corn's shucked
and the beans snapped. And the clarity
of that calling: one syllable issuing in
the long wide sweep of our old
life. It rings down from a high
porch step, and her fingers about to go
into her mouth so she can whistle
for me, which she'll do next,
if I don't turn now and nod
that I've heard her, that I'm coming.

Baby & Brain

The baby beams to see
how the model of it opens
when the professor hands it to her.
Its snap-together compartments
should keep her amused
for a while. And Oo, oo,
what's that wad in the middle?

She tugs it, sniffs it, taps it
as the professor tells her mother
about the psychology of failure.
Obviously she hasn't learned it,
having bombed the last quiz,
and isn't it high time she got
her priorities straight?

The baby smacks together
the two bright orange hemispheres
in a way that would make any real brain
give up its ghosts. Under tiny pigtails
the baby squeals. She claps her hands.
At their late semester impasse, the professor
frowns and the mother fumes.

The tightness of her pigtails *hurts
her brain,* the baby will say next year
to the mom who's still busy
and has to hurry the baby's hairdo.
Already the one tail wants to stand up
to pain, and the other to avoid it,

to shake itself out in a wind.

But for now, two lobes, all purpled
and tangled by impossible nerve-ways,
go high-stepping across the floor.
Then the baby puts one
into her mouth. And *Stop, don't
eat that,* the mother says.
We don't know where it's been.

Miniature

On top of the ice planet and through a window
we look out at figures on sticks in the snow—
colorful hotdoggers headed downhill in a hurry.
Hurry! A tour bus of the world is about to depart.

We sip what's warm in our cups. The display
is crowded, confused. For how many thousand years
have they wrapped themselves like this, like mummies,
and stood at the summit, counted 3,2,1, over and out.

Centuries slip like mantles of snow off neighboring
mountains, but down the adventurers go, calling past
their worries—Oh what's a little thunder—and off
the glittery perimeters of the moonlit globe.

Our magisterial hands: huge in regal shadows
raising darkness to our lips. If only all this watching
had not left us at the precipice of exhaustion,
we might go to the cupboard for a black dropcloth

to drape the whole scene. Or if the scene itself were not,
in its kindly chaos and of its own accord, so lovely,
we might suffer our hands to lift and shake it, but only
gently—just enough to start the big flakes falling.

Cockadoodledo
(Woman Selling Dogs in the Village)

Some dogs don't love a looker
even a little. But if a man's browsing,
the smart pup will give his ankles a sniff,
lick his shoes clean. Though I'm what
they love a lot, the one the cock crowed

into rising, into going ahead,
laying the trail of pitiful chow.

In this town everyone sleeps late.
A tireless wind
in their night-wear, and how tardily
their fields are sown.

Once a man's language and mine
intersected across 17 words. No three
made a sentence. No two finished
a thought. But it furthered us to have
somewhere to go—even just a dot, dot, dot.

Nothing was ever wild among us
but the weeds in my shoes.

Now that man is awake
and rowing. Always the first
to rise. His forearms heave
and release a weight of water.

Later, hot sun on the market, the dogs will lie
in the shade of only me. I'll let loose their chokes

but they won't go far. Spotted hound for the Baker.
Black spaniel for the Vicar. Such affections: negotiable
currency, pocket change for my many pockets.

The bitch setter gets up, circles
her pup, backs off when it tries to nurse.

Come evening I'll have been so long away
from my plot of black beans,
I may finally decipher the yelps
and yaps of the dog tongues.

The more they say, the more they confuse
each other. *Shush* is what we know best—
all of us resolved in the one mind of patience.
Morning, then noon, slip toward a wide
river. The rower slides in and out of view.

How heavy the water must be
to pull his face so far away.

And how light is the water remembered
and thrust back. Seventeen words of a song
mimic the oarlocks clicking, echo
lovers far off in time in a creaky bed.

There she goes. Looking for a home on her own.
Good dog, last of my goldens, she runs
upriver and down, follows a boat's
black shadow. She's dizzy and shivering
and eager to greet the man

who wants to stop rowing, to steer
the boat back through the froth of dreams.

On the bank, the pup runs—frantic, barking
at the oars. Wagged into the mud
are her thousand exclamation marks.
She's this new to love, this anxious to please.

Unfinished Canvas
(Flemish Peasant Family)

No wonder the Antwerp teashops
refuse him—except with a heel of bread
through the back door. Held out
to the baker, his palms, still sticky with paint,
hardly appear the hands of a man.

The four lives he wanted to lift
only obliquely to his canvas
have waylaid his backward glance.
An elbow rip for the boy's shirt sleeve
takes all day. The swift forwardness slows.

He cannot make the man in the cap appear
his father exactly, though the woman's
hard glare has dropped from above
the very breast he suckled. Such looks
take their long passages through him.

Once he liked to sip strong wine. Now nothing
is too strong going through but the light.
July's sundown so late it shortens a night's
dreaming: chins & ankles, tatters for a man's
cap brim, grime for a woman's petticoat hem.

Eating bread, standing up in the cobblestone
alley, he thinks Shoes, yes for the boy,
but not for the daughter. From her eyes'
other side, get the shine turned up:
the blue rosaries of misgiving.

The temptation to make them all meek,
swarms of Mary's. Once this bread went
into its red cave, and came out the color of noon.
So a child's expression veers off. Toward sweet
smells: steam through the vent grates.

Here, let this pale doughy heel be finished,
erased by the body. Rarely saving the strength
to be gentle. Flecks of pity, rubbed raw, smear
into bewildered Joseph's: hunched and addled,
ripping a dove's breast loose from its back.

Sometimes to look as the worm looks—
the no one's view of everyone. Or to see
as the startled sparrow—from high and fleeing
on the wing. A dab at the mother's eye, as if she's
through sobbing for her prodigals, her runaways.

A single drop of black goo opens, expands
her gaze. Soon the falls of her secret blood
begin to blast their spray. Then yes, to stand
in that spray—stroked by it and stroking,
soaked to the bone and singing.

Two Hungers. John the Baptist.

Some days my followers won't wait.
But when the lizards stop sizzling
we know they're done.
Some things we can do

we don't even know. The body
translates the mind. Chooses
the word that's stuck
and offers its own version.

Though the versions I prefer
are full of fasting. Turn
the sticks, and the lizards,
our friends, go belly up.

Some nights, like them I sleep
with my back to the fire.
Ah, I say, to be *of* the fire
but not *in it,* not quite.

I keep my two deserts secret:
one that's the Jordan's floodplain;
her madmen swirl about me, and the faith
of no man's father reeling.

And my wide other one, empty
under the sun. I crawl to it
naked, embrace its warm rocks,
offer the prayer in its tongues.

Our House Was Full without Us

Dew all morning, and the trees are crystal towers
    till noon. They circle the sagging tents
and cardboard oven boxes in which strangers

stir in their meadow of dreams.
    Strangers: they fill up
the blue bowl of this valley. And stranded,

laid out in our basement—the unnamed;
    along our hallways—the never known before
or seen. All whom we do not disturb.

We shut the door and walk up to the ridgetop.
    Below us was once a field of labor: hay
sown and mowed, then the dozen horses of autumn

prowling yellow stubble, all winter their backs
    to the wind. Mornings now, the dots of fires
start up. New birds on our acres of air,

and lately a violin on the inward breeze.
    Bigger flames, darker wings,
and larger sighs of sound.

* * *

Star-spangled, the strangers in the evening
    are a wonder of words.
A small bell rings, and someone's saying:

On the sixth day of Genesis, the animals'

first-pronounced breaths filled the air
with a great wilderness. Neither yet a wind

to fear, nor a thunder. Mewed and baahed,
    the separate psalms set out alone
upon the gathering airs of night.

*   *   *

I see when an afternoon breeze dies down
    a blanket I'd mended long ago: rows of
running horses stitched back awhile to our world.

Their manes, fiery chevrons; eyes fixed by a fury,
    one by one. A holy bell in the branches,
it rings, and the low clouds course.

The darker the nights, the more the fisher bats
    hover above the river: splash and squeal,
and the more ripples on the water.

The Queen's Concussion

The mother's blue robes, so heavy, have caught
her heel. One daughter's on the top step,
and one's on the bottom. A tough rain outside
tears the last leaves off the aspens. Before
their mother was blue-robed and magisterial,
men paid dimes to dance with her, and then
a war began. Dimes stock-piled for a peace.

Dancers all, the soldiers had never heard
the work-song that spilled out when a geode
cracked open on their path of blood. Inside it
was a crystalline city. For centuries its little men
had hammered to get to this sudden light,
never dreaming the ache of it, the way
it could wind their eyes back into black.

* * *

Watching her bleed into the stairway's bend,
the mother's two most loyal subjects wept.
The bone that had held them all roundly,
that had dismissed noisy leaves troubled
by rain—now it dripped a slow stream. The girl
on the bottom step, who had read Tu Fu,
waved back unfed dragons from the door.

Upstairs, the other girl called for a priest
to scatter incense on the ten thousand airs.
So a whirlwind began. It sucked the last dimes
and the castle's spirals into the red vortex
of a stairway with a woman crumpled there:

her head-wound the gaping hole into which
framed ancestors leapt and roof tiles flew.

* * *

Before the war she'd had no subjects. She'd
been a simple woman in a black hat with a veil
to conceal her eyes' sparks. When a needle
went down on a song like a pickax on a stone,
her high heels lifted her into a swarm of arms.
She spun a nation toward disaster. Dimes flared
as the leaves do now—bright and pummeled by rain.

Her subjects call for a light to look farther
in there, where even the ancient scraggly men,
even the crippled, maimed, and loony men
labor for peace in a frenzy. There's the maze
they've hacked behind, and the dense luminous
crystal up ahead, and someone deep down
with his hand on a detonator the size of an atom.

Rookery

1.

He's our Mercury, our pheasant, stepping under
the hand-clipped hedge with a satisfied
whistle-toot. At home in the woods,

and from all he's pecked into his bright body,
his body's making supplies. Sun hung up
in the low pines—then gone

with another toot toot blasted. We can't
be certain if it's the day that ends
this way, the century, the world.

2.

We rowed until we couldn't heave our oars
one more yard. Upstream in a murkier version
of the Phasis River, two groups—

the hymnists and the phrenologists—lay back
in the wet of each other's arms. They'd
dropped all their shoes on shore

so that not a single extra pump could have
squeezed its way in, nor another foot
found its toehold in the water.

Upriver was a muggy air, and we, unlike
the revelers, could hardly breathe
through our cathedrals of ribs.

Ah, to be so unleashed, unwasted: the chosen singing

the chosen's verses, counting skull bumps
of the never to be forgotten.

3.

All week the river had been turning over,
churning up what had lain on the bottom—
cleaning itself. Roiling, as if a message

were trying to get through: a random flood,
full of a very hot something, was headed
for the rookery. River birds, squawking,

dropped a cuneiform scat on the shore.
Through the minds of their predecessors
a scene, illuminated by white feathers

of frost, was unreeling. We didn't know
what began like this—a morning,
a next life, a homeless rowing.

Every Good Thing
(Stele of Cheywath)
250 B.C.

Famished under the stone. The lips, sealed
tight, still taste, but lock down a hunger.

His cleaned-out body—and laid before it
a thousand of bread, beer, oxen, fowl,
and every good thing. His gratitude
is the breeze over the stone.

Hieroglyphs say who he was
with extinct birds, half-risen suns.

Now, and with only a few brown figs left
in their sack, robbers poke a hole in the crypt.
Ravished by heat, they've journeyed far.
Wearing the wrong shoes, dripping sand.

The wealth of their new lives is heaped
at this table of the dead. But where to sit?

They stand. The last fig pits fall
among the gold and the bones.
And in the way a thief cloaks his face,
the final breeze cowers and backs off.

The courtier's mourners, hot from baking
and slaughtering and crying, filed by.

It was all right in that millennium
to touch him, envy his calm and his cool,

and to pat his belly which was full already
from so much feasting on the other side.

Nance Van Winckel teaches in the graduate creative writing program at Eastern Washington University. She is the author of two books of poetry—*Bad Girl, with Hawk* (University of Illinois, 1988) and *The Dirt* (Miami University Press, 1994)—as well as two books of short stories, both with the University of Missouri Press: *Limited Lifetime Warranty* (1994) and *Quake* (1997). A recipient of a National Endowment for the Arts Poetry Fellowship, her poems and stories have appeared in such places as *The American Poetry Review, The Georgia Review, The Nation, The Ohio Review,* and *The Paris Review.*